LIFE IS A TRIP

For information address

J2B Publishing LLC
4251 Columbia Park Road
Pomfret, MD 20657
www.J2BLLC.com
GladToDoIt@gmail.com

Printed and bound in the United States of America

ISBN: 978-1-948747-50-9

LIFE IS A TRIP

Richard I. Gold

J2B PUBLISHING

Also by Richard I. Gold

God's Agenda: Religious Poems - Vol. I

Mary's Lamb and other Christmas Poems

God's Love - Easter Poems

Sayings for the Believer

Work is a 4-Letter Word

Free Advice

Dedication

My thanks to my wife who has helped me with the initial review and to those who have reviewed this work over time.

Table of Contents

This book has a collection of poems about life as we may travel it. Some of the poems may be a little humorous, others serious, but many have some application to life.

1. LIFE IS A TRIP

Life is a trip
A one way trip
A one way trip on a train
And you have a ticket
A ticket to ride
A ticket to ride on that train

The train is so fast
So fast beyond belief
That though there are troubles
There comes no relief

The ride goes through times
Troubles come your way
But you can be very sure
For your evil you will have to pay

You've left the station
You're on the train
Remember
If you get off
You can never get on again

2. TINY HANDS

Tiny hands
Tiny feet
Oh my child
Looks so sweet

Looks like an angel
Sent from God
Hope you grow
To give me a nod

Yet tiny hands
Tiny feet
Grow to adult
To rule the street

3. THE LECTURE

The lecturer stood so upright and proud
He talked to students in a voice both soft and loud
His talk of economics was so technical and deep
The students were puzzled and almost put to sleep

Finally the professor interrupted to explain
What the great lecturer had said to all
"If your outgo exceeds your income
Your upkeep will be your downfall."

4. THE SPEAKER

I've come to tell you
The speaker said
The future is yours
Don't harbor dread

The future may be beautiful
Or so very, very dark
It may be hard and dreary
Or it may be a lark

It depends upon you
On how you understand
The things you learn
Will help you stand

Study what you are given
Study hard, study deep
So that when you apply for a job
A job you will keep

5. JOHN MARLEY

John Marley, the name on the bust
Nothing else is said
There is a likeness
Of shoulders connected to a head

His thoughts, his deeds
When he walked the land
Was he loved or hated
When he lived as a man

His intelligence
Lay behind the eyes
His personality
His likeness belies

All we know of his history
The deeds he had done
Are what others have written
Of his life now gone

6. MY BROTHER

My brother was a living pain
To those with whom he lived
It was not that he was evil
But that he was enslaved

When he was very young
He learned that having things
Was pleasant to himself
And did, he thought, pleasure bring

Then one day a friend of his
Said "Here, try this joint, bud
You will be cool and popular"
Then he was hooked on crud

He lost his way, he lost his love
He lost his future too
But ere he was hooked
There was nothing he could do

He lived many years
Brought his mother pain
Sometimes drugs would keep
Sometimes made him insane

Then he did something wrong
He knew that he should not
And by the law
He found himself caught

He did not do the right
Pleasure was all he did desire
He walked on the wrong side
Got caught in passion's fire

He took his life
To keep out of jail
He thought the inside
Would be a living hell

And now he's gone
Dead before his time
He could have led a useful life
But died in his prime

7. EPITAPH

A cemetery is a dismal place
Filled with the dead
Although it'll someday be our home
It should not fill us with dread

On each grave there is a stone
An inscription may say
Some witty comment
To those who pass that way

On my stone I wish to have
A saying I hope is true
That will have applied to my life
And to my memory too

"When I am dead and gone
I hope that men will say
'Here lived a man
Great in his day'"

8. JUSTICE

The world is full of right and wrong
Let no one you deceive
But often the final justice of an act
Is in how you perceive

The justice of a deed
Comes from what we believe
Has happened and has been done
And what we perceive

But the justice one desires
Is not the same for all
It is a factor we grasp
As through life we fall

It is built on what we believe
What we think we know
Justice can be quick and fast
Or it can be very slow

Matters what a man believes?
Or yet a woman too?
It does not change the facts
But changes what we do

9. THE SPEAKER

"I'll keep it short"
The speaker said
"I'll not bore you
With what I've read"

Well, short is relative
It depends upon the speaker
But the audience observed
The time was a sneaker

The subject was interesting
But the speaker was a bore
Before it all ended
You could hear the audience snore

10. REMEMBER

In a million years
A million years and a day
When all the possessions we work for
Are destroyed by fire, mold, and decay

When our lives are gone
Our names forgotten too
What will remain
Is the good and evil we do

So go forth and do good
To those both great and small
That when we are judged by our Maker
We will be loved by all

11. THE PATH OF LIFE

You walk along the path of life
You do not know the end
Along the way you may meet a lover
Who may also be a friend

You walk that way but once
You can never return
Nor retrace your steps
No matter how you yearn

A lover is a lover
Who may or may not be true
But a friend is a friend
Who will always be true to you

So we have lovers
Both old and new
But the desirable thing
Is to have a friend so true

Thus we should marry a lover
Who will also be our friend
Then they will be with us
To help us to the end

12. A BILLION DOLLARS

If I had a billion dollars
A billion dollars and a dime
It could buy me many things
But could not buy me time

Money can buy clothes
The house I own
But it cannot buy love
Nor make my house a home

But love is in the giving
Of myself and my wealth
It is in the helping
That will be my eternal health

13. MAKE NO PROMISES

Make no promises you will not keep
Make no commitment you wish you had not
Make no pledges that through your being seep
Nor vows that will cause your soul to rot

But through your life hold steady
To the principles you know are true
Let your bonded word be known
That what you say you will do

14. THE FLOWERS OF SPRING

The flowers of spring and the leaves of fall
Are beautiful in their way
They reflect God's sunlight
Affect us as they may

The flowers are a beginning
Full of promise, hope and trust
The falling leaves are the ending
Of things completed, of things we must

So it is with our lives
We flower when we're young
But with the passing time
Our race we will have run

15. WORK IS THE FATE

Work is the fate of men
And of women too
It keeps us out of trouble
Gives us something to do

We do not work only for gain
Although this is a goal
But for the satisfaction of work
Which is what we hold

To be useful to others
Is one's chief desire
But when we feel we're used
The consequences can be dire

So, my son, go forth and work
From sun to setting sun
That when your life is over
You will have something done

16. GEOMETRY

Geometry is a study of shapes
The configuration of lines
It proves that things are so
It boggles the mind

There are shapes in life
That are not on paper drawn
They are there for us
Although the reason on us does not dawn

There are restraints in our work
In our social life also
And we are expected
These lines to know

When we cross these lines
Violate some social rule
We will be given the cold shoulder
By those who think us a fool

If we cross the wrong line
Go our own way
We will find in fact
There is much we must pay

17. BUMPER STICKERS

Bumper stickers are a scourge of man
They sit so pretty and still
Telling some statement of thought
That the driver will

Sometimes they are designed
To build and reward
Sometimes they have the effect
Of causing great discord

The stickers which are worse
Are those that result
They are short and makes a point
That causes an insult

But at times the message
That the driver doth send
Is a different message
That they do not intend

"He who dies with the most toys wins"
Is a message of greed and spite
It says that the owner will step on you
And not do you right

"If it's too loud, you're too old"
The message does proclaim
The lack of good taste
Apparent all the same

"Who says I don't lift a finger"
With a vulgar sign
If the person were to break down
They would have a hard time

There are many other bumper stickers
That give a message loud and clear
But if the owner were to pay the price
The price would be dear

18. EVERYTHING HAS A PRICE

As we go through life
We often interact
With other people
That is a fact

When we interact
When they do us good
Something we must repay
We know we should

How do we repay the friendly smile?
The opening of a door?
We can repay with a kind word
And go on as before

We show our appreciation
Can sometimes give money - yet
If we do it with a mean spirit
It does not discharge the debt

If we wish the action to continue
If we wish them to do us good
We must repay kindness with kindness
Do what we know we should

A simple smile, a wave of thanks
Will go a long way
We will discharge simple debts
Which we should, come what may

For larger measures of help
For those who do us very good
We must write a note
And do what we should

19. THERE ARE THINGS

There are things
That make them "they"
Things that divide
For some it is her or him

But you might ask
Who are those that are "them"
This is a difficult task
Because if you have to ask
You are one of "them"

20. THE IMPERATIVE THEREFORE

There are many things
That the speaker would have us do
They give many arguments
Some false, some true

Of the actions we should take
Of the reasons for us to act
They present many arguments
Some a little short on fact

The speaker says that A is true
So it is with B
Therefore because of these
We should do C

Yet if we know C is wrong
We should be able to say
This is not my way
Not the price I will pay

For the actions we do
Are ours alone
If we do the bad
For this we must atone

So consider what is asked
Consider what you should
And be always guided by mind
To do what is good

21. TRUST

Trust is a precious thing
Built by word and deed
It depends upon being consistent
On answering those we plead

As long as trust exists
It makes itself real
Makes the trustor
Build upon the ideal

But when trust is fractured
Then it is totally gone
For where there is not trust
There is not a trusting one

22. THE WHEEL OF FORTUNE

The wheel of life grinds on
It moves through space and time
There seems to be no direction
No reason, no rhyme

When we win, when we lose
It seems to be in the hands of the "odds"
It is determined by the wheel of fortune
Rather than the hands of the gods

It is the wheel of fortune
That guides many a life
Determines the present and the future
Determines if a woman becomes a wife

But fortune cannot be worshiped
It is not a thing
But the interaction of events
That to us the future bring

23. EAST AND WEST

East is east and west is west
And never the twain shall meet
But they all agree
Everyone has to eat

The things that divide us
Are rooted in the past
The things that make us one
Are the everlasting task

The task that makes us one
Is the human need
It is the mercy and justice
For which we plead

Governments that do not give
But crush the very will
Are systems and governments
That can only fail

Sometimes the wait for justice
May seem interminably long
When it is the ruling system
That was used to do wrong

There may be not promise
Now, for a better life
But we can forever struggle
In this world of strife

For the future is forever
The present is but a passing phase
The eternal tomorrow
In heaven we will sing praise

24. RIGHT AND WRONG

Some people believe in Heaven
Some people do not
Some don't believe in Hell
Some believe that it's hot

Some people believe in doing right
Others believe in getting what they can
Some people don't believe it matters
As long as they win

Whatever we believe
We believe it is correct
And we will follow
Whenever it does connect

But does it matter what a man believes
Or yet a woman too
It does not change the facts
But changes what we do

25. THEY SAY

They say they want the truth
That is what they say
If the truth flatters them
They will be willing to pay

But if the truth is not flattering
If it exposes their warts
You'd best be prepared for the worst
Because, as they say, the truth hurts

26. THE COMPUTER VIRUS

Smuk was a good computer programmer
The best that there could be
But the things he liked to program
Were computer viruses, you see

He could write a virus
That would data destroy
He could make the instructions
That added many a ploy

He could hide viruses in the system
So that nothing could detect
And make it pop out
Whenever it chose to infect

He got a kick out of destroying files
Upon which businesses depended
He could see top executives squirm
As stockholders upon them descended

His viruses went everywhere
Data he did destroy
He did not worry
The results he did enjoy

One day his program got into medical records
But he could not care
Until he got very sick
And his records were not there

And then he died
His records could not be recovered
Now, he could not be buried
No trace of him can be discovered

27. CONFLICT

There is disagreement
And there is discord
All this conflict
Is a distort cord

Sometimes conflict is bad
Or it may be good
It depends on how it is used
On what our outcome should

So sow the seeds of conflict
There's a wide range
For within every conflict
There are the seeds of change

28. THE GATE KEEPER

A sunset upon the waters
An idea of what to do
We watch others
To determine what is true

Many are the things we do
To keep separate unto ourselves
We want to be alone
Like Santa and his elves

To go between ourselves and others
Between the outer and inner part
We have a gatekeeper
That gatekeeper is our heart

29. ON WINNING

There is winning and losing
And how you play the game
There are accolades for the winner
Losing is not the same

When you win it feels so good
You could just walk on air
When you lose you feel so bad
You could cease to care

But winning and losing are not final
They don't define the game
In the future you remember
They both will be the same

The object should be winning
Losing is a shame
But you will find the importance
Is that you played the game

30. THE WISDOM OF THE AGES

The wisdom of the ages
Is written, spoken, and told
From old to young throughout time
But sometimes from young to old

Wisdom is a beautiful thing
Desirable in every way
But it is something we must want
To keep and help us know what to say

31. AS I WAS STANDING BY THE DOOR

As I was standing by the door
There came a knock, demanding
A knock and nothing more
As there I was standing

Do I open the door, do I let it in
There was another knock
Do I pretend I am not here
Do I keep the door locked

Who is there
For my good or for my bad
When I open the door
Will I be happy or sad

But open it I must
For I am standing here
The future is coming in
The future is out there

We must all make decisions
On what we will do
The future is in our actions
May be just and real and true

32. THERE IS MANY A WORD

There is many a word
That we have heard
That leads us to distraction
And many a thought
We have brought
That leads us into action

There is one word
Have you heard
And that word is work
And we can find
To do what we mind
If we do not shirk

This is the point retort
Of this poem short
That we find meaning in the doing
If all thoughts be true
It is what we should do
The doing is better than the talking

33. THE WAY WE SHOULD LIVE

There is a way we should live
To know wrong from right
We may not get ahead
But at least we can sleep at night

When we do what is wrong
Knowing that it is not right
We can go on living
But lose our way to the light

What is the way to live
What is it we should do
Many people have asked that question
They only wish that they knew

The way is hard but simple
To give and not to get
To love those about you
To pay your just debt

The way of the saint is harder
It is something that you know
To deal justly with others
Love your neighbor as you love you

34. LONELY PEOPLE ALL ALONE

Lonely people all alone
Offer souls to their friends
Very seldom do they cross
Any barrier that offends

Yesterday is a shadow
Of things gone by
Until we are able
Return again and try

Lonely people among friends
Often find their joy
Voting with their presence
Enter in without a ploy

Lonely people all alone
Must find things to do
May what they find be right
Be peaceful and just and true

35. LONELY PEOPLE

Lonely people
All alone
Need someone
To call their own

Lonely people
Who need a friend
Someone who is there
Faithful to the end

A friend becomes a lover
A lover becomes a friend
Each needs the other
To be loved to the end

Love your love
With a love so true
And your love
Will love you too

36. THE TATTERED FLAG

The tattered flag
Sits on a hill
It is defended
By those, there, still

For what purpose
Are those, there, staying
It is their goal to stay
The price they are paying

For most people
There is not an actual hill
But there are objectives
That fits the bill

We all have objectives
That in life sets our goal
In it we have a reason
That makes our life bold

But as with the hill
And with the tattered flag
There should be a reason
Else life is a drag

Goals are our objectives
And obtaining it is a thrill
But if we have no objective
We have no hill

37. MEETINGS

Meetings are a fact of life
We often cannot escape
We are drawn into their orbs
As over a chair we drape

Those who run the meetings
Have agendas all their own
We sit and listen
Weary to the bone

Some meetings are long and dull
They can often be a bore
But ere you fall asleep
Be careful not to snore

38. WHERE ARE YOU GOING

"Where are you going?"
A question to ask
If you know the answer
You can set your own task

If you know your destination
If you know your direction
You can aim for that end
Without deflection

Unfortunately, this is often not the case
We find that we judge progress
By the speed, not the direction
And may in the process, regress

So know where you are going
In life as in each day
Your life will be lived
You will succeed on life's way

39. DESIRE

Desire burns hot
Within the breast of man
But desire given wings
We would do what we can

What is it you desire
What is it that makes you go
Often it is being human
A wind through your life does blow

The winds of passion are strong
If not held in check
Will blow your soul away
And make your life a wreck

But passion and desire
Can build a life also
Make us what we should be
As through life we go

40. INTEGRITY

Integrity is a ten dollar word
A word we all desire
In those with whom we deal
No matter if the results are dire

Each of us has integrity
Upon which our reputation depends
If we compromise ourselves
Scorn upon us descends

Some buy and sell others
Making them do their will
By money, drugs or threats
Always a bitter pill

Once you've sold your integrity
You've sold your soul
You cannot buy your freedom
You cannot be made whole

41. THE INTERVIEW

The interview for a job
Is a foot in the door
You need to sell yourself
That is your chief chore

If you would be employed
Get the really good job
You have to look your best
Don't be a slob

42. WHEN WE WENT TO SCHOOL

When we went to school
We learned to read and write
We learned to do our numbers
But did we learn wrong from right?

For right and wrong must be taught
From every passing day
We will fall into error
If we do not know the way

So let us learn the lessons
From the sage of old
That when our life is judged
We will be judged to be gold

43. BITTEN BY A MUSE

John was an ordinary guy
Ordinary in every way
He could do many things
Throughout any day

He could think good thoughts
Keep his side of any conversation
But he could not write
Or make a poem by convention

Then one dark and stormy night
When the lights were down low
He got bitten by a muse
That was quite a blow

He started to write
He could not seem to stop
All day, all night
Until he was about to drop

When he was through
You should have seen his output
It made "War and Peace"
Look like a notebook

When he was through
His real work did begin
He tried to sell his book
The work of mind and pen

From one publisher to the next
John went to and fro
He visited each one
But finally didn't know

His book was finally published
Printed without a flaw
By a small company
Owned by his brother-in-law

44. DELEGATION

Everyone has a job to do
Tasks that must be done
Many details to cover
A program to run

The bottom line is results
In the least money and time
Consistent with quality
The goal is prime

Often there are many tasks
More than anyone can do
So parts must be delegated
To get results, this is true

So if you have many tasks
You must assign parts
And trust someone else
To work it with their heart

But the guidance is yours
To get the job done
This is your project
Your project to run

For failure you may blame others
For this not does ring true
For in the final analysis
The results are up to you

45. INSPIRATION AND PERSPIRATION

Inspiration is what we think
Ideas that we have had
Without inspiration to guide
Our efforts could go bad

Perspiration is what we do
Develop ideas to the end
This is where the work
Where the problems begin

Without inspiration
Our work is in vain
Without perspiration
Inspiration just causes pain

46. SUCCESS

Success is getting what you want
Throughout life's fleeting time
It is what we all seek
In all that we have in mind

Happiness is wanting what we get
To make do with what we have
To know that we need less
It will contentment give

To get what you want
To want what you get
To do both is good
When we've achieved it all, and yet

We go through life
Looking for the golden ring
We grab at what we see
But maybe it is the wrong thing

As we work, as we climb
The ladder of success
We often find
Not happiness, but stress

So often we get
What we think we want
But when it is in hand
We often find we don't

But true happiness
Is wanting what we get
And when it is in hand
We have the best life yet

47. THE PROBLEM OF EVIL

The problem of evil
Is that it is bad
Without this evil
A much better life is had

As we live our life we often wish
That some divine force
Would destroy evil
Making things better, not worse

Sometimes we say
"If God be God
Evil would be
Dead beneath the sod"

If the Divinity has power
Power that is absolute
The Divine would stop evil
Right now, give it the boot

Sometimes this evil
Is in what we see
It is not in the eternal
That it has come to be

Sometimes we find evil
As payback for what we do
Results of our actions
To standards we were not true

Often it seems evil comes
Not from what we do
But by the laws of chance
Even if we have been true

But evil is not
So much an absolute
As it is in doing wrong
To things that are mute

Look to the standards
Of wrong and of right
That you will do good
With heart and with might

We cannot stop evil
In the world as a whole
But we can stop evil
In what we control

In all, the question of evil
Is an absolute mood
The way we are judged
By the standards of the good

48. STANDARDS

We work and strive
We do right, not wrong
Sometimes we sell ourselves
For little more than a song

We sell what we have
For a moment of pleasure
Then we live to regret
In the time of our leisure

To keep on a steady course
That will help you succeed
You need a goal, a standard
Bad actions to impede

So set your standards high
Also your goal
So your life will have meaning
And yourself will not be sold

49. THE CITIZENS ARE ABOUT

The citizens are about their business
They are busy in every way
I would I were so employed
On every golden day

For we do not works for others
A profit for to make
But they must be ready to give
Much more than they take

For if we work for others
Doing as little as we can
We make ourselves replaceable
By many another man

We must work for ourselves
A product to make
For we may be paid by others
But it is our reputation that's a stake

50. LINES IN OUR LIVES

There are lines in our lives
That we dare not cross
Lines that make us who we are
They keep us from loss

Lines of morality, of faithfulness and of love
That keep us safe and warm
That does not us destroy
But keep us from harm

But when we cross those lines
And venture out to see
We often find that where we are
Is not where we want to be

So when the results come in
And find we are in a fix
We have only ourselves to blame
Because we wanted to get some kicks

ABOUT THE AUTHOR

Richard Gold was born in Bartow, Florida and attended college and worked for the Government for 40 years. He has been a Christian and writing poems for as long. Gold is now retired which gives him the time necessary to continue to write. Gold lives in Indian Head, Maryland with Penny, his artistically talented wife.

www.ingramcontent.com/pod-product-compliance
Lightning Source LLC
Chambersburg PA
CBHW032214040426
42449CB00005B/592